GOODWILL'S

Essays and Stories

For Primary Classes

Indu Gupta

GOODWILL PUBLISHING HOUSE®

B-3 RATTAN JYOTI, 18 RAJENDRA PLACE

NEW DELHI-110008 (INDIA)

Published by:

GOODWILL PUBLISHING HOUSE®

B-3 Rattan Jyoti, 18 Rajendra Place
New Delhi–110 008 (INDIA)
Tel: 25820556, 25750801, 25755559
Fax: 91-11-25764396
E-mail: goodwillpub@vsnl.net
goodwillpub@gmail.com
ylp@bol.net.in
Website: www.goodwillpublishinghouse.com

Printed at : Kumar Offset Printers, Delhi-110092

CONTENTS

ESSAYS

STORIES

ESSAYS

1 MYSELF

My name is Mary Jane. I am 10 years old. I live in Singapore. My family consists of my father, my mother, my younger brother and myself.

I have long brown hair. I love to play with my dolls, listen to music and read fairy tales.

I have many friends in school with whom I play during my lunch break. My class teacher is very nice and polite. She helps me to understand and learn my lessons easily.

My father is a policeman. He works very hard from morning till night. My mother teaches in a school. They both love me a lot. My brother is still too young to go to school. He stays with the nanny till my mother comes back home. Being the baby of the family, he is everyone's favourite.

My father takes us to the amusement park whenever he gets time off from his work. Every Sunday my mother cooks a tasty lunch and we all sit to eat it together.

I thank God for giving me a loving family and a wonderful life.

2 My Mother

My mother's name is Lily. She is very beautiful. She dresses up very well, and her smiling face makes her look very pretty.

She is very hardworking. She gets up before sunrise and is the last one in the family to go to bed at night.

She takes care of the household chores

such as cooking, cleaning, etc. and helps us with our homework. She tells us interesting stories every night before we go to sleep.

She is a very good painter. Whenever she gets time, she paints lovely pictures. She also teaches me and my sister how to draw.

She plays piano very well. I love to listen to her when she is playing. She also gives piano classes to children in the evening. I am proud of my mother. I hope to be like her someday.

3 My Father

My father's name is Peter. He is thirty-five years old. He is an architect and runs his own company. He makes sketches of big buildings. He is a very hardworking man. He goes to his office at eight thirty in the morning and returns home at seven in the evening.

On weekends, he takes us out for picnic and movies. He plays different games with me and also helps me with my homework.

He is a good sportsman. On Sundays he plays tennis with his friends. He also teaches me how to play the game. He goes jogging every morning, and takes me along with him on weekends.

He is a very kind and honest person. He believes in discipline. He listens to my problems very patiently and helps me to solve them. He helps my mother with household chores.

I love him a lot, and he is my greatest strength.

❀ ❀ ❀ ❀ ❀ ❀ ❀ ❀ ❀ ❀

4 My Family

I have a small family. My family consists of four members—my parents, my brother and myself. Our lovely house is in the middle of a small town.

My brother and I go to the same school in the neighbourhood. I love him a lot. We have common friends with whom we play.

My mother is a very good cook. She takes bakery classes in the town. My father works in a factory. He is a very hardworking man. Even though our parents are tired after they come back from work, they always help us with our studies. They also tell us stories and play games with us. We have lots of fun at home. We always have dinner together.

On weekends our parents take us to the nearby city. I love to go to the city, as we have loads of fun there. I love my family a lot.

5 My Neighbours

I live in a small colony in Brisbane. Mr & Mrs Spencer are our neighbours. They are very nice people. Mark, their son, is my best friend. We go to the same school. He is of same age as me and we spend a lot of time together.

Mr Spencer is a lawyer, and his wife is a teacher. They are respected by all in the neighbourhood. They live a very simple life.

They are kind people who are always ready to help others.

Whenever I am alone at home, Mrs Spencer looks after me. On my last birthday, she baked me a delicious cake.

Mr Spencer and my father go together for morning walks. We also go out for holidays together. They are always fun to be with.

My mother and Mrs Spencer go to the market together. At times they take me and Mark along.

They have a beautiful garden. Mrs Spencer loves gardening. There are different kinds of flowers in their garden. I love to walk and play with Mark on the soft grass.

A good neighbour is a blessing. I love my neighbours as they are with us in moments of joy and sorrow.

6 My Hobby

Like all my friends, I too have a hobby. My hobby is coin collection. I started collecting coins nearly a year ago when my father gave me coins of different European countries. He had also bought me an album for keeping the coins.

At present I have nearly 150 coins with me. This collection has taught me a lot about various countries across the world.

I love to spend my free time with my coin album. My mother told me that this hobby of coin collection is known as Numismatics. She too helps me in collecting different coins.

I have coins of different shapes and with different languages written on them. My elder brother helps me to learn more about the coins that I have collected. Some coins are very old while some are new. Some coins have figures of kings and queens, others show animals on them.

I am proud of my coin collection. I keep it very safely in my cupboard. I show it to my friends and also share my knowledge with them.

7 My Favourite Pet

My favourite pet is different from that of my friends. On my seventh birthday, my father bought me a little goldfish. We kept it in a glass bowl on my table. Since then it has been my best friend.

I call my fish Goldie. It is very beautiful. It has a golden tail and lovely fins. Its big black eyes are a treat to look at. It swims in the bowl like a mermaid.

I share all my secrets with my goldfish. I make sure that I feed it on time.

When I go to school, my mother looks after it. I miss it a lot when I am not at home. All my friends love it too. I wish I could play with it more often and take it along with me wherever I go. But I cannot take it out of water.

My father has promised to buy a big aquarium for Goldie, as it has grown too big for its small bowl.

I hope Goldie will be happy in its new home. I also want to get some more friends for it, so that it does not feel lonely when I am not at home.

8 My Best Friend

My best friend's name is Albert. I call him Al. We go to school together. We study in the same class. He is good at studies. Many a times he helps me to understand my lessons. After school we do our homework together.

In the evening, both of us play with our other friends in the neighbourhood. He does not fight with other children; instead he is always ready to help them.

He stays in my colony and is an excellent baseball player. He is a simple boy belonging to a small loving family. Besides his parents, he has a younger brother. We visit each other's house frequently. We also go swimming together with our parents.

I met him two years back. We share our happiness and sorrow with each other. His hobby is to learn different languages. He knows Spanish and has taught me to speak a few sentences in Spanish.

I am happy to have such a wonderful friend.

9 My School

My school is very big and nice. Its name is Mount Fort High School. It is not very far from my house. It has big buildings and green fields.

Hundreds of students study in my school. Our uniform is white and blue. There are one hundred fifty rooms in my school. We have a gymnasium, a swimming pool, a music room and a dance room. Our art room has beautiful paintings on the walls. We have a very big library which has a wide variety of books.

All our teachers are polite and highly educated. Our principal is a very kind and loving person. We are like one big family.

My school conducts various competitions. Our teachers encourage us to participate in extra-curricular activities. We are taught yoga, horse riding, swimming, skating and many other sports in our school.

It is always fun to be in school. I love my school a lot.

10 My Favourite Teacher

My class teacher is Mrs Monika Lewis. She is a very kind and loving teacher. She is a middle aged lady who has a motherly affection towards her students.

She teaches us English and history. She often tells us interesting stories about the past. She never gets angry, instead she calmly explains us our mistakes.

She tries to make our lessons interesting and fun to learn. Sometimes when the weather is pleasant, she takes us out in the school garden. She also accompanies us on picnics and school excursions.

Last month, she took us to see an ancient castle. There she showed us how the kings and queens lived in the olden days.

Although she never punishes, she believes in discipline. She visits her students whenever they fall ill. She always tries to help us out when we are in trouble. She makes us feel as if our school is a second home.

She is my favourite teacher and I always look forward to her classes.

11 MY CITY

I live in Toronto. My city is famous for the Niagara Falls. It is a beautiful city. It is located in Canada, North America. Apart from the famous Niagara Falls, my city has many different things to see. It has beautiful art galleries, gardens, museums and theme parks.

It is a very large city. It has many big and busy roads. In summers, Toronto is warm and full of festivities. During winters, it is very cold and chilly.

The people in my city are very loving. They love to go for skiing during winters and camping during summers. People from across the world have settled here.

All round the year tourists come to visit my city. The eleven museums in Toronto tell us about the history of the city. The CN Tower is the most famous monument of my city. It is located in the Front West Street.

I love my city a lot. I am sure there is no other city in the world where I can live so happily.

12 My Dream

All of us dream of becoming famous when we grow up. My dream is to become a pilot. One day I want to fly a big airplane.

On my last birthday, my father gifted me a toy plane. I wish I could sit inside it and fly high up in the sky.

I love the big aircraft at the airport. It really excites me when I think of flying like a bird in the sky. As a pilot, I will be able to fly above the white clouds and travel around the globe with different people.

I am ready to study and work hard to fulfil my dream of flying high among the stars.

With my mother's help, I have made a big collection of different models of planes. Some of them are small, some are big, and some have fans on their head.

I would like my mother and father to be the first ones to fly with me when I become a pilot.

I am proud of my dream. One day I shall fulfil my dream and become a pilot.

13 My Favourite Sport

My favourite sport is basketball. I live in Melbourne, and basketball is a very popular game in Australia.

Basketball is played between two teams. Each team has five players. Points are scored by throwing the ball into the basket fixed at each end of the court. At the end, the team with more points wins the game. It can be played indoors as well as outdoors.

Usually this game requires very tall players. Players should be fit, with strong arms and legs.

I am a good basketball player and enjoy playing this game very much. I am the captain of the basketball team of my school. I also play the game with my friends in the neighbourhood. I love the game so much that I would like to play it for my country when I grow up.

14 My School Library

My school has a very big library. It is on the ground floor of the school building. It has hundreds of books. It has books on all subjects. It also has a number of storybooks and magazines.

Inside the library, there are rows of tables and chairs. Big cabinets are kept all around the library. Books are alphabetically arranged in these cabinets.

Students of all classes visit the library as per schedule. We all have library cards which we carry to school every day. We can borrow one book at a time from the school library.

Our librarian is a very nice lady. She has

a lot of knowledge about books. She makes sure all books are returned to the library on time. She maintains the library very well. Many a times she helps us in locating and selecting books.

I love to visit my school library, as this is one place where I can sit and study peacefully without any disturbance.

15 MY CLASS PICNIC

Last month our class teacher took us for a picnic. It was a lovely experience.

We went to a garden near our school. We were asked to carry some food. Some of us carried fruits, some carried cakes, and some carried snacks. We also took along bats, balls and other games.

In the morning, we boarded our school bus and left for the rock garden. Once we reached there, our teacher helped us to select a comfortable place to sit. After eating fruits, we played lot of games. Our teacher also played with us. After that she took us for a walk round the garden.

In the afternoon, we were all hungry and tired. We sat together and had our lunch. Then our teacher read out lovely stories. We all sat together listening to her. After an hour she took us back to the bus and we all came back to the school.

I will never forget this picnic, as this was the first time that I went for a picnic with my school friends and had great fun.

16 A VISIT TO THE ZOO

Last weekend, my father wanted to take us out somewhere. So we decided to go to the zoo. My mother made some sandwiches and packed some fruits. Father took his camera along, and we all left for the zoo.

Outside, it was warm and sunny. After an hour's drive, we reached the zoo. The place was crowded. There were vendors selling balloons, caps, eatables and lots of other things.

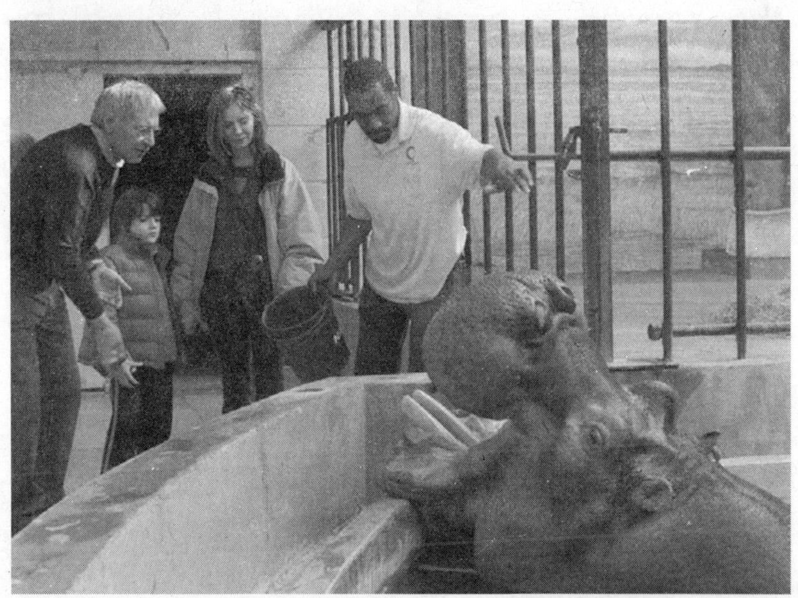

My father bought three tickets and we all walked into the zoo. Inside we boarded a small train which took us around the park. I was so excited that I kept jumping on my seat.

As the train moved slowly around the park, we saw a lion, a white tiger, hippopotamus, deer, giraffes, mongoose, bison, wolves and hyenas.

After the train ride, we sat in a restaurant and had our lunch. While walking around the zoo, I saw boards which warned us not to feed the animals. I could not understand the reason behind it. When I asked my father about it, he explained that our food might harm the animals. He also told me that the zoo authorities take care of the animals in the best possible manner.

After lunch, we left for our home though I wanted to stay back and go for the train ride again.

17

A Visit to the Museum

Last summer when my grandfather came to visit us, he took me to the museum. The visit was an unforgettable experience. It was the first time that I had gone to such a place.

My grandfather has great knowledge about history. On our way to the museum, he told me stories of the kings and queens of our country. Inside the museum, he showed me many things. There were big swords, shields, daggers and other weapons with which the kings used to fight. He also showed me the rich dresses and ornaments of kings and queens. I also saw their coins and other articles.

Everything we saw had a story to tell. My grandfather told all the stories to me. Seeing those things, I felt as if I had landed in a different world altogether. We came back home after a few hours. My grandfather has promised to take me to another museum next time he visits us.

18 Our Local Market

We have a small market near our house. It is our local market. Though it is not very big, one can buy almost everything there.

The market place is always crowded. The shops are mostly small in size. Some shops sell fruits and dairy products, some sell groceries, some sell fish, some sell utensils, some sell gift items and stationery. One can also find shops selling electronic goods. There are shops for repairing damaged things also.

In the middle of the market there is a big

medical store. It has all kinds of medicines available.

There is also a nice bakery shop just outside the market. It sells delicious cakes

and cookies. I love to go to the market as my mother buys me goodies like candies and cakes.

My mother goes twice a week to the market to buy various things.

This local market has made our lives very easy as all day-to-day items are available at a comfortable distance. The shopkeepers are honest and sell quality products at reasonable prices.

19 A Visit to the Airport

I live in a small town near Longford in London. Last Sunday, my father had to go to the Heathrow airport to receive his uncle. He took me along. I had never seen an

airport before, so I was very excited to go with him.

We reached there in the afternoon. The entire place was buzzing with people. Outside the airport, there were cars and taxis. People were rushing around with huge suitcases and bags. Everyone seemed to be in a hurry!

I could hear loud roaring sounds coming from the sky. My father explained to me that the sound was due to the landing and take-off of the airplanes.

As we entered the airport, it seemed like a different world. I almost screamed with excitement when my father showed me huge planes near the runway. I wanted to sit in one of those big planes.

My father assured me that one day we will definitely fly to another city in one of those airplanes.

20 A Post Office

Post offices are found in every city, town and village.

A post office is a very important place. It charges a nominal amount for carrying our letters and parcels from one place to the other. It helps us keep in touch with our friends and relatives, who stay in far off places. We can send registered letters, birthday greetings, parcels and money

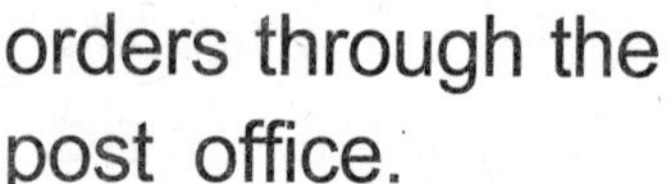

orders through the post office.

We post our letters in the letter boxes outside the post office. The postman collects these letters and sends them to their destination. The postmen work day in and day out. We must respect and appreciate their hard work.

Although there are many new methods of communication nowadays, the post office is still very important. Nothing can compare to the joy we feel upon receiving a postcard from a friend on a holiday or a card to wish us a happy birthday.

21 MY COMPUTER

My computer is very special to me. I got it as a birthday gift from my parents last year.

My computer has a monitor which looks like a television screen. It has a central processing unit. It also has a mouse which is used to move the cursor. It also has speakers.

With my mother's help, I have learnt how to type words using the keyboard. I have also learnt how to draw pictures on the computer. With the help of my computer, I am able to do my school projects quickly. I am able to gather a lot of information on various topics from internet, and make beautiful projects. My father showed me the Seven Wonders of the World on the computer screen through the internet. It was truly amazing!

Sometimes, with the help of my parents, I chat with my cousins staying in other countries. We also send pictures and letters to each other through email. I want to learn more about computers and make the best use of this wonderful birthday gift.

22 A Visit to My Grandmother's House

Every summer vacation, my parents and I go to visit my grandmother. This time too we went to stay with her for a week.

My grandmother stays in a small town near Berlin.

Her house is very beautiful and it is located in the middle of the town. The house has four bedrooms and a huge kitchen. This time when we went to meet her, I found her lovely garden full of beautiful flowers.

She was very happy to see us. We stayed with her for a week, and each day she cooked something special for us. She also baked my favourite chocolate cookies.

The weather there was very pleasant. So one day we all went for a picnic to the lakeside.

At night I slept in my grandmother's room, and she told me lovely stories. She not only showed me my father's pictures when he was young but also narrated many funny incidents about my father and his friends.

She gifted me two pullovers which she had knitted herself.

I always feel happy to be with her. I wish I could stay with her for a little longer. I left her house with a heavy heart. She too felt sad about us going back. We promised to visit her soon.

23 A Scary Night

I still remember that dark and gloomy night. It was raining heavily outside. As I was scared to sleep alone in my room, my mother stayed with me till I fell asleep.

Then suddenly a strange noise woke me up. I found myself alone in the room. I gathered courage and opened my eyes to look through the window. The only thing I saw was a strange shadow dancing near my window with its eyes wide open. I started screaming with fear.

My parents came running to my room and found me crying. When they asked me, I told them about the strange noise and the shadow.

After listening to my story, my father looked outside the window and started laughing. He hugged me and holding my hands brought me near the window. I was still very scared to look through the window.

Gathering courage, I opened my eyes and looked. What I saw, made me laugh too. It was the old tree outside my window. Its branches were making the noise because of the strong winds outside, and its leaves were forming the dancing shadows. As for the eyes, they belonged to an owl sitting on the tree!

I felt very foolish. I promised my parents that I would be braver and stronger in future.

24

AUTOBIOGRAPHY OF A TREE

I am a mango tree. I live in an orchard. Though I am old, I am still very strong. I have many branches which are always full of green leaves. I also bear fruits. My fruits are known as mangoes. They are very sweet and juicy.

I was very small when I came to the orchard. The gardener has been looking after me since then. He gives me water every day. With time I have become tall and

strong. Now I look after him. When he is tired, he comes and rests under my shade. I feel very happy when he takes some mangoes home for his children.

I have many friends in the orchard. Some are old like me. Each of them bears a different type of fruit. Children love us. They come to play in the orchard every evening. They swing from my branches and hide behind my trunk. They love my fruit. I feel really happy to see them playing around me. But when they pull out my leaves just for fun, I feel great pain. I wish their elders could stop them from doing so.

25 The Brown Horse

My uncle has a horse who runs like the wind. My uncle has named him Malibu. He is reddish brown in colour. He has two little ears. He is very tall and the most beautiful one in the stable. He eats grass and fodder.

He is a gentle horse and children love to ride him. Malibu can work very hard. Sometimes he carries heavy loads on his back.

My uncle takes him for a walk every day. He can jump high across a fence and run very fast. At night he sleeps in the stable with other horses.

My uncle takes very good care of Malibu and the other horses. He gives them healthy food and keeps the stable clean. Every week, the vet comes to the farm for their checkup.

When I go for a visit to my uncle's farm, I always take a ride on Malibu's back. He takes me around the farm. When I grow up, I wish to have a horse of my own like Malibu.

26 MY BIRTHDAY PARTY

It was my eighth birthday. My parents gifted me a red bicycle and arranged a big party for me. The house was decorated with streamers and balloons. A special birthday cake was ordered for me. It was a chocolate cake, with juicy cherries on the top.

My grandparents came from Montreal to attend my birthday party. All my friends were also invited. I was very happy to see them. They all brought gifts for me. My mother kept them carefully in my room.

We all wore nice party dresses. My friends blew on whistles when I cut the cake.

After cutting the cake, we played many games. My mother gave prizes to the winners. We then had our dinner.

After dinner, my parents gave gifts to all my friends. My father went to drop them back home. It was a lovely evening. I loved each moment of it.

27 IMPORTANCE OF ELECTRICITY

Electricity is generated with the help of water, coal and even sun rays. Electricity is very important for us. The lights in our houses glow with the help of electricity. This light helps us to study at night. Electricity

helps to light up the streets at night. The appliances our mothers use to cook food work with the help of electricity.

It is electricity that makes our refrigerator, geyser, television, mobile phone work. It is also used to run trains from one place to the other.

Electricity also helps us to play video games, listen to music and play with electronic toys.

In our modern life, we cannot do without electricity as it helps us to use various man-made luxuries such as heaters, ovens, computers, etc. We should not waste electricity because resources to make electricity are scarce and will not last forever.

28 CHRISTMAS

Christmas marks the joyful celebrations of Jesus Christ's birth anniversary on 25th December. People of all religions enjoy and celebrate Christmas with full zest.

Christmas is one of my favourite festivals. I eagerly wait for it all through the year. We do lots of shopping, markets also wear a festive look with special Christmas cakes, pastries, toys, Christmas trees etc. on sale.

Before my school closes for Christmas vacations, I give gifts and cards to my friends and teachers.

On Christmas eve, I buy a Christmas tree and decorate it with stars, glitters, noels, lights, candy sticks. I hang up my stockings on Christmas tree hoping that Santa Claus will leave a nice gift for me, though I know my parents put those lovely gifts inside my stockings when I go off to sleep at night.

On the Christmas day, my parents gift me something special. I also give them gifts that I buy with my pocket money. We visit friends and relatives and exchange gifts with each other. We go to the church to offer prayers and enjoy singing Christmas carols. I wish everyone a Merry Christmas.

My mother prepares our favourite dishes and lots of pancakes, puddings, pastries, pies for the special Christmas dinner.

With the new year in offing, Christmas sets in high spirits for the festive mood.

29 VISIT TO A HILL STATION

Last winter, our family went to Simla, a famous hill station. It was the first time that I had visited such a nice place. It was very beautiful and peaceful.

We went by car and it took us eight hours to reach Simla. We reached there at three in the afternoon and it was very cold. We checked into a hotel and had our lunch. In the evening, we went for a walk on the Mall Road. The place was full of small and pretty houses. The local people were very friendly. They even offered us tea.

The next morning we went to the famous spot, Chail. It was a place from where we could see the entire valley. I had never seen such a beautiful place, and so I was very excited. I clicked many pictures there.

We then went to a nearby market. The place was full of people from different countries. My father bought me few picture postcards, and my mother also shopped a bit. We left the place early next morning. I loved the place so much that I would like to visit it next year too.

30 My Red Toy Car

I have a beautiful red toy car. It has four wheels and two doors. It has two big headlights.

My grandfather gifted me this car last Christmas. It is my favourite toy. It runs on battery and plays soft music when it moves.

My car is remote-controlled. Using the remote control, I can move the car backward and forward, open its doors and switch on the headlights. My car can run at a very high speed. My friends love to play with my car. They say that it's the fastest toy car they have ever seen.

I take good care of my car, and after playing with it, I keep it safely in my cupboard.

31 A House on Fire

One night, as I was sleeping, I heard loud cries of "Fire! Fire!", I got up and saw our neighbour's house on fire. I rushed out along with my parents.

Everyone in our neighbourhood was out and trying to help put off the fire with water

and sand. Thick smoke was coming out of the house.

Soon the fire engine came. It was a big red vehicle. The firemen got down to work immediately. They sprayed water on the house. Some firemen asked us to move away from the house. After an hour's effort, they were finally able to control the fire.

Everyone in the house was safe and only one portion of the house was damaged. We asked our neighbours to stay with us for the night. It was such a scary experience that none of us could sleep that night.

32 A Cold Winter Night

This winter, I experienced the coldest night of the season. It was six in the evening and cold winds were blowing strongly outside. The water was icy cold, and made my fingers numb.

We all decided to stay inside the house. As the night grew it became colder. We wrapped ourselves in warm clothes and sat in front of the fire. I was wearing three pullovers, but was still shivering with cold.

My mother made hot tomato soup for us. It was great to have the hot soup, as it made me feel warm. Around nine at night, it started snowing heavily. Looking outside the window, I saw snowflakes falling on everything. It made me shiver with cold all the more. I could hear the strong icy wind blowing outside. When I felt scared, my mother held me tightly. In her arms, I felt warm and soon dozed off to sleep.

33 A Visit to the Forest

My elder brother is a forest officer. Last week, he took me with him to the forest. I was thrilled and excited, as it was the first time that I was going to the forest. He had told me stories about various animals. I hoped to see some of them.

It was early in the morning when we started for the forest.

Inside the forest, there was very little sunlight. I was excited yet scared. It was very quiet. My brother told me not to make any noise. I sat quietly next to him. After driving through the forest for half an hour, my brother suddenly stopped the jeep. He told me to look to my left. There in the bushes I could see a herd of deer. I was overjoyed.

I wanted to go near them. But my brother said that they would get scared and run away. He also said that it was not safe to get off the jeep. We also saw an elephant, a peacock, a litter of cubs and some fluffy little rabbits.

An hour later, we came back to our house. I was so happy that I gave my brother a tight hug.

34

My Brother's Wedding

Last month, I went with my family to attend my cousin brother's wedding. The venue was looking beautiful with flowers and lights everywhere. All arrangements

had been made. All of us were very excited and came dressed in lovely clothes. Light instrumental music was being played. My brother wore a smart suit and tie. He was looking very handsome.

In the wedding hall, I sat next to my mother. After sometime the bride came. She was looking very pretty. Her white gown made her look like an angel. She was carrying a big bouquet of flowers in her hands.

After the wedding ceremony, the food was served. My brother and his bride sat with us to eat. After lunch, we bid them goodbye and returned home.

35 ELEPHANTS

Elephants are the largest land animals on earth. They are either black or grey in colour. They have four legs and a small tail. Their ears are big and they have a long and powerful trunk.

They use their trunk to drink water and pick up food. They have two large white teeth known as tusks which they use for their protection. They also have small teeth inside the mouth.

Elephants eat fruits, shrubs and grass. They love to eat sugar-canes. Elephants are very strong and powerful. At some places, they are used to carry heavy loads. Elephants live in herds. They look after their young ones just like our mothers do. They laugh, play and cry like we do. They are also known to have a very good memory.

36 DOLPHINS

Dolphins live in oceans. They are mammals who belong to the family of whales. They have three fins and a beautiful tail. They use their tail for swimming. They have a pair of eyes and a pointed beak. They also have teeth.

Dolphins love to eat fish. They communicate with each other using sounds like clicks and whistles. They live in groups called pods and are very playful by nature. They love and protect their young ones. They are known to be friendly and intelligent by nature. They are also kept in water parks and tourist spots to perform tricks. They are fast learners.

37

The Sparrow on My Window Sill

A little sparrow comes and sits on my window sill every day. Every morning, I hear its chirping. I have named her Birdie.

She has a beautiful white neck, two wings, a small tail and a tiny beak. Birdie is light brown in colour.

Every night I keep a handful of grain on my window sill for Birdie. Birdie eats grains,

fruits and insects. She has built a small nest on the roof outside my room. She has built the nest with twigs and leaves. I wish I could build her a strong bird house.

My mother says she is soon going to lay eggs. I am waiting for the little young ones to come. Birdie and I have become real good friends. I wish I could play with her like I do with my other friends.

38 WATER

Water is very necessary for us. All living things need water to survive. Water is found in oceans, rivers, lakes and ponds. We also get water from rains. Water of the ocean is salty and not suitable for drinking. We can drink water from rivers and fresh water lakes. We also find water in the form of snow.

Water is used by us in our everyday life. We need water for drinking and bathing, for

cooking food and washing clothes and utensils. Plants and animals too need water to survive.

Farmers need water for cultivation. It is used in factories. It is also used for generating electricity and building houses. Water is needed everywhere. We should neither waste nor pollute water as each drop of water is precious.

39 Our School Peon

Our school peon's name is Jack. He is a middle aged man. He is very tall. He has grey hair and a thick moustache. He wears a white uniform to school. It is always neat and clean.

He reaches school before us to clean and arrange our classrooms. During the day, he works very hard. He carries books and other important papers from one class to the other. He also takes letters from the school to other nearby offices. When we get hurt, he takes us to the school doctor. He looks after us and also takes care of the school garden.

He tells us stories when we do not have a class. He stays back after the school gets over and leaves after locking up all the rooms. He is a very nice man. We all love him a lot.

40 TAJ MAHAL

The Taj Mahal is located in Agra, India. It is very beautiful. It is one of the wonders of the world. It was built by Shah Jahan, a Mughal Emperor, in the memory of his dear wife, Mumtaz Mahal. This is why the Taj Mahal is seen as an eternal symbol of love.

The Taj Mahal was built many years ago. 20,000 men took twenty-one years to build it. It is made of white marble. People from around the world come to see it. There are beautiful gardens in front of the Taj Mahal. It has four minarets around it. The gate to enter the monument is made of red sandstone. Although the beauty of the Taj is breathtaking at all times of the day, yet on full moon nights it looks splendid.

41 My Daily Routine

I get up early in the morning. After I wake up, I wish my parents. I then go and brush my teeth. I have a bath and dress up for school. I then eat breakfast with my parents. After breakfast, I go to the bus stop to catch my school bus.

I reach school at eight in the morning and attend my classes. At midday, we have a recess. I eat my snack with my friends and play games with them. After recess I get back to my class. I return home at two p.m. and then take my lunch. After lunch, I take a nap and then finish my homework.

In the evening, I go to play with my friends. I come back home and finish my lessons. At eight o'clock we have dinner. After dinner my father tells me stories. I go to sleep at ten o'clock. Before going to sleep I brush my teeth and wish my parents 'goodnight'. This is my daily routine.

42

Try! Try! Till You Succeed

This summer my father taught me how to ride a bicycle. It was not easy to learn. I was very scared in the beginning. My father used my elder brother's bicycle to teach me how to ride. It took me seven days to learn. But I am happy that I could learn riding at last.

My father took me for practise every day. But I was unable to get over my fear. On the second day when I still could not ride, I started crying. It seemed very difficult, as I kept falling.

My father told me never to give up. He said we should keep trying till we succeed. So, I plucked up courage and started learning again. Though I kept falling, I did not give up. My father was with me all the time. On the seventh day, I could ride the bicycle all by myself. I was very happy. My father hugged me and said he was proud of me. He also gifted me a new bicycle.

That day I learnt one important lesson. We should never give up. No matter how hard the task is, we should keep trying till we succeed.

43 A DROWNING BOY

This summer, I took swimming classes with my friends. We had a trainer with us. One day, we were all sitting near the pool after the day's session. Suddenly we heard a cry for help. We turned around and saw a little boy struggling in the pool. The boy did not know how to swim. He had accidentally fallen into the pool.

Some elder people were sitting on the other side. One of them jumped into the pool. He held the boy tight and swam to safety. We all helped the man to pull the little boy out of the swimming pool.

The boy was crying and was very scared but was safe. We wrapped him in a towel and asked him to relax. Fortunately, a big tragedy was avoided that day.

44 LOOK BEFORE YOU LEAP

We should always think about the results before we say or do something. We should always think carefully before acting. This will keep us from getting into any trouble. Some people do not think before they speak or do something. This lands them into trouble all the time.

It is important to know about the possible outcome and dangers before we say or do something. We should always ask our parents before we decide on something. Advice from elders always helps us to make up our mind. Elders have better knowledge than us. It is always good to discuss with others before we do anything. It helps us to know the results of our actions. If we do something without thinking about its outcome, it can harm us.

45 A Cricket Match

Last Sunday, I went with my father to watch a cricket match in the stadium. It was a one-day match between the teams from Calgary and Halifax. A large number of people had come to see the match. After waiting for thirty minutes, the umpires came to the field with the captains of the two teams. The coin was tossed. The captain of the Calgary team won the toss and decided to bat first.

Soon, the match started. With every run that was scored, the supporters of the

Calgarian team clapped and shouted. The team from Calgary made 200 runs and were all out. Now it was the turn of the team from Halifax to perform. In the lunch hour, my father bought lemonade and sandwiches.

The match resumed with Halifax team batting. They played well but could not score 200 runs. There was cheering from the supporters of the Calgarian team. People blew whistles to celebrate the victory of the first team. I also kept clapping like others in the stadium. I loved watching the cricket match. It was a thrilling experience.

46 OUR SOLAR SYSTEM

There are eight planets in our solar system. The Sun is at the centre, and the planets revolve around it. Mercury, Venus, Earth, Mars, Jupiter, Saturn, Uranus and Neptune are the eight planets. The path of the planets is known as an orbit.

Mercury is nearest to the Sun. Neptune

is the farthest planet. Jupiter is the biggest planet among all of them. Saturn is the only planet which has rings around it.

The Earth is the third planet from the Sun. It is the only planet on which life exists. It has one natural satellite, the Moon. Jupiter has 63 moons. Saturn has 60 moons. It has some of the largest moons in our solar system.

The galaxy in which our solar system lies is known as the Milky Way.

47 GOOD MANNERS

Good manners are very important for a happy life. A civilised person will always behave properly with everyone.

Every morning we should wish our elders. We should also pray to God for a good day. In school we should always wish our teachers. We should always give respect to our elders and teachers. We should never fight with our friends; instead we

should be polite, helpful and friendly towards everyone.

We should neither speak ill about others nor use harsh words for anybody. When someone helps us, we should always be thankful to that person. It is our moral duty to help all those who are needy and helpless.

Before going to bed at night, we should always thank God for everything He has given to us.

48 The Night Before the Examination

Last week I had my final examinations. I always feel nervous before the examinations. I had studied hard the whole year. I had finished my syllabus, but I was still very worried.

One week before the examinations, I had studied extra hard, but I was still frightened the day before my examination.

It was Sunday. I had my mathematics examination the next day. I had studied the whole day. I had revised my syllabus twice. But at night after dinner I started feeling very tense. I wanted to sit and study again, but my father told me to stay calm and go to sleep. I went to my room to sleep. After an hour or so, I woke up and went to my parents' room. I started crying with fear. I told my mother that I do not remember anything. She took me in her arms and held me tight. She took me to bed and told me that I will remember everything when I wake up the next day. I felt protected with her. I

slept peacefully. The next day I went to take my examination. It went very well. As my mother had said I remembered everything. I went home and thanked my parents for all the support.

49 The Army Men

The army men play a very important role in our lives, as they protect our country. They ensure that no enemy enters our country from outside. They sacrifice their lives for the sake of the nation.

They undergo intense training before they join the army as soldiers. They leave their families back home and work hard for protecting the borders. They are posted in different parts of the country. They live a very difficult life. They sometimes have to endure extreme climates.

At times of war they are the first ones to come forward and fight for the country. Even at times of flood, famine and earthquake, they come forward to help the people of their country.

They are the true protectors of the nation and our lives. We should always respect them.

50 OUR BODY

Our body is a wonderful creation of God. Nature has assigned different tasks to different body parts. We chew with our teeth, see with our eyes, hear with our ears, feel with our skin, walk with our legs and so on.

All the body parts and organs work in co-ordination with each other. If we neglect any body part, then the whole body suffers.

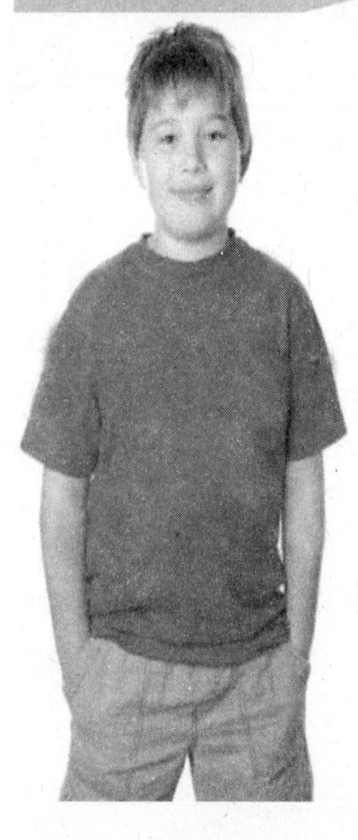

Inside our body there are many systems. We have a digestive system which helps us to digest all the food we eat to give us energy to work. Our heart beats all day and all night. It beats faster when we run or walk fast. We can feel our heartbeat if we place our hand on the chest. We have a pair of kidneys. They are as important as the heart. They help to clean the blood in our body. We also have a pair of lungs which help us to breath. We have a brain inside the head which controls all the other organs of the body.

We must take proper and good care of our body since a healthy mind can reside only in a healthy body.

51 FRESH AIR

Fresh air is very important for us. We can live without food and water for some time; but not even for a few minutes without air. We cannot see air. It is a mixture of many gases.

Without air our planet would be lifeless. Fresh air is very important for plants and animals too.

Nature provides fresh air to us through plants and trees. So plants and trees help to generate fresh air. In cities, the air gets mixed with harmful gases from factories and vehicles. This polluted air makes us fall ill.

We should plant more trees to keep the air fresh. We should not throw wastes everywhere. We should try and keep our surroundings clean. This will help us to live a healthy life. We should protect forests from being cut down. We should all join hands to build a greener and healthier environment.

52 A Rainy Day

It was very hot this summer. There was no sign of rain. But one day when I was in school, dark clouds appeared in the sky. It started drizzling as school got over. We were all very happy to get relief from the hot scorching sun. Hardly anybody had their umbrellas or raincoats with them that day. After sometime heavy rain started pouring down. When I reached home, I was thoroughly drenched. But I was feeling great.

The smell of wet earth was very refreshing. I sat near the window to watch the rain. The

streets were flooded with water. I made small paper boats. In the evening when it had stopped raining, it became very cool and pleasant. My friends and I went outside to float our boats. I wish it rains more often.

53 The Farmer

A farmer's job is to plough the fields and sow the seeds. When the crops grow, he harvests the crop and sells them in the market. His job requires a lot of hard work.

A farmer lives a simple life. He wakes up at dawn and goes to the field. There he works for the whole day. After the sun sets he returns home.

He grows different types of crops for us. During summers he grows rice, cotton and

jute. During winters he grows peas, potatoes, wheat, etc. He also provides us with sugarcane, cabbage, cauliflower, beans and many other vegetables and grains. We get all our cereals and vegetables from the farmer's field. He provides us with the food we eat. It is only because the farmer works so hard that we get our food so easily.

54 SEASONS

World is very vast and every part of it has a different climate. However, the most prominent seasons are summer, winter and rainy seasons.

Different parts of the world experience different seasons at different times of the year.

Seasons change according to the earth's revolution around the sun. During a year, as the earth revolves around the sun some parts of the earth face the sun and receive more heat energy from the sun. Hence,

these parts of the earth experience summer. At the same time, the parts of earth which are not facing the sun receive less heat energy, hence, experience winter. That is why at a given point of time, some parts of world experience summer and some winter.

Some parts of the world do not get very cold, mostly because of the influence of the sea. As the winters start fading away and the heat begins to intensify, people pack up their woollens. Out come the sun-shades, umbrellas and cotton clothes. Sale of ice creams and soft drinks becomes a regular feature during scorching summers.

Between winter and summer seasons, there is a short period called 'spring'. When

spring sets in, flowers burst into bloom and the earth seems to be smiling. During rainy season, raincoats and umbrellas are

constant companions. As the showers fade away, once again winter sets in. Thus, goes on the seasons cycle.

We enjoy each season with its fruits, festivals and weather.

55 IMPORTANCE OF MILK

Milk is an important part of our daily diet. It has great nourishing value. We should have milk every day.

Milk is not only important for growing children but also for people of all age groups. It is a rich source of calcium, protein, fat and vitamin C.

We get milk mainly from cows and buffaloes. Other animals that give us milk are sheep, goat and camel. We use milk in our everyday cooking. Milk is used for making tea and coffee. We also use milk to make yogurt, cheese, cream and chocolates. We get milk in dehydrated powder form also.

It is very important for babies to have milk. It makes bones stronger and gives us energy. It is also good for improving memory.

56 Biography of a Fruit Vendor

John is a fruit vendor. He sells fruits in the market. He is a kind and humble man. He has a small shop where he works from morning till night.

He sells different types of fruits such as oranges, pineapples, bananas, strawberries, blueberries, apples, grapes and many more. He also sells seasonal fruits as mangoes. All his fruits are very fresh and juicy.

He loves all kids who come to him. He tells them short stories about the fruits. He also tells them about the countries from where those fruits come. He tells them how important the fruits are for a healthy body.

He lives in a small cottage near the market. He has a small garden where he grows some fruits. Everyone loves him.

57 CEREALS

Cereals are a very important form of food for us. They are the staple food in our diet.

The major cereals are rice, wheat, millet, oat, maize, barley and corn. All these cereals are produced in farms.

We consume cereals in different ways. We have them for breakfast in the form of cornflakes, bread and cakes. During lunch and dinner, we have cereals in the form of rice, wheat and whole grains. We also eat cereals in the form of popcorns.

Cereals have a great nutritional value. They contain vitamins, minerals and fibres which give us energy to work. They form a healthy part of our diet. We should have them every day. Having cereals every day would keep us away from many illnesses.

58 CALENDARS

Calendars are very important for us. We use calendars to see dates, days, weeks and months. We also use them to see the upcoming festivals and carnivals. A year is divided into twelve months. They are January, February, March, April, May, June, July, August, September, October, November and December.

CALENDAR

JANUARY					
MO		7	14	21	28
TU	1	8	15	22	29
WE	2	9	16	23	30
TH	3	10	17	24	31
FR	4	11	18	25	
SA	5	12	19	26	
SU	6	13	20	27	

FEBRUARY					
MO		4	11	18	25
TU		5	12	19	26
WE		6	13	20	27
TH		7	14	21	28
FR	1	8	15	22	29
SA	2	9	16	23	
SU	3	10	17	24	

MARCH					
MO	31	3	10	17	24
TU		4	11	18	25
WE		5	12	19	26
TH		6	13	20	27
FR		7	14	21	28
SA	1	8	15	22	29
SU	2	9	16	23	30

APRIL					
MO		7	14	21	28
TU	1	8	15	22	29
WE	2	9	16	23	30
TH	3	10	17	24	
FR	4	11	18	25	
SA	5	12	19	26	
SU	6	13	20	27	

MAY					
MO		5	12	19	26
TU		6	13	20	27
WE		7	14	21	28
TH	1	8	15	22	29
FR	2	9	16	23	30
SA	3	10	17	24	31
SU	4	11	18	25	

JUNE					
MO	30	2	9	16	23
TU		3	10	17	24
WE		4	11	18	25
TH		5	12	19	26
FR		6	13	20	27
SA		7	14	21	28
SU	1	8	15	22	29

JULY					
MO		7	14	21	28
TU	1	8	15	22	29
WE	2	9	16	23	30
TH	3	10	17	24	31
FR	4	11	18	25	
SA	5	12	19	26	
SU	6	13	20	27	

AUGUST					
MO		4	11	18	25
TU		5	12	19	26
WE		6	13	20	27
TH		7	14	21	28
FR	1	8	15	22	29
SA	2	9	16	23	30
SU	3	10	17	24	31

SEPTEMBER					
MO	1	8	15	22	29
TU	2	9	16	23	30
WE	3	10	17	24	
TH	4	11	18	25	
FR	5	12	19	26	
SA	6	13	20	27	
SU	7	14	21	28	

OCTOBER					
MO		6	13	20	27
TU		7	14	21	28
WE	1	8	15	22	29
TH	2	9	16	23	30
FR	3	10	17	24	31
SA	4	11	18	25	
SU	5	12	19	26	

NOVEMBER					
MO		3	10	17	24
TU		4	11	18	25
WE		5	12	19	26
TH		6	13	20	27
FR		7	14	21	28
SA	1	8	15	22	29
SU	2	9	16	23	30

DECEMBER					
MO	1	8	15	22	29
TU	2	9	16	23	30
WE	3	10	17	24	31
TH	4	11	18	25	
FR	5	12	19	26	
SA	6	13	20	27	
SU	7	14	21	28	

Each month is divided into weeks and days. There are seven days in a week. The seven days are:

Sunday,
Monday,
Tuesday,
Wednesday,
Thursday,
Friday and
Saturday.

There are four weeks in a month. Some months have thirty-one days while others have thirty days.

April, June, September and November have thirty days. Only February has twenty-eight days. In total there are three hundred and sixty-five days in a year. In a leap year, February has twenty nine days and the year has three hundred sixty six days.

By letting us know the date, the day and the month, calendars help us to plan our work. Different countries have different calendars. Some countries follow lunar calendars and others solar calendars. We cannot live a well-planned life without the help of the calendar.

59 Books—Our Best Friends

Books are our best friends. Whenever we are alone, books can become our best companions. We can read books for fun and to gain knowledge. Books help us to know about a lot of new things. Whenever we have a doubt, books can help us out. There are different types of books. Some books have stories to tell us, and some have new things for us to learn about.

We learn about animals, plants and birds from the books. Books tell us about places and people of far away countries. They also teach us good manners and ways to lead

a good life. We should read good books whenever we get time. We should take good care of our books. We should not dog-ear, tear or spoil our books.

60 THE METRO RIDE

Yesterday my mother took me for a ride in the underground metro. It was a thrilling experience as it was the first time that I was travelling in a train that ran under the ground. There were many people at the metro station. All were rushing from one platform to the other. I held onto my mother's hand tightly, because I was scared of getting lost.

We reached the platform. After a few minutes our train came. We all stood in a queue and waited for our turn to enter the train. Once everyone had boarded the train, the doors closed automatically. I was amazed to see this. In a very short time we reached our destination. My mother helped me get out of the train. Even this station was bustling with people. They were all moving towards different trains or the exit.

As we came out of the underground metro station, the bright sun rays hit my eyes. It was warm outside. I wished I could go back and take the metro ride again.

61 My New Haircut

Last Sunday, my father took me for a haircut. After the barber had cut my hair, I felt like crying. He had cut my hair very short. I was very sad. When I came back

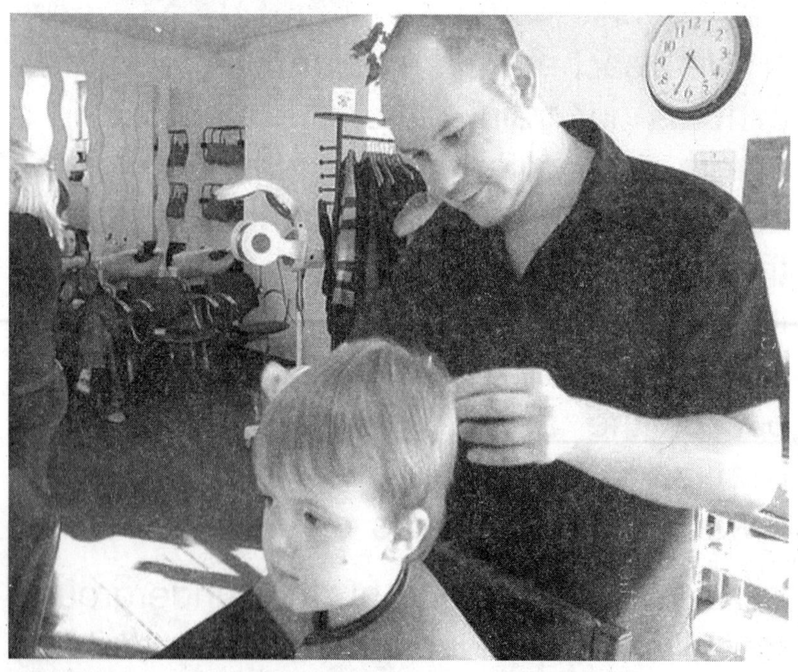

home, I stayed in my room the whole day. Seeing me sad and unhappy, my mother got worried. When she came into my room, I started crying. I told her that I wouldn't go to school with that haircut. I thought all my friends would laugh at my new haircut. My mother is very kind and understanding. She told me not to worry. She embraced me and said that my new haircut was looking nice on me. I felt good and confident on hearing this.

Next day, when I went to school, all my friends told me that I was looking nice in my new haircut. I felt foolish for crying the previous day. I was happy that my mother was there with me when I needed her.

62 My Favourite Cartoon Characters

My favourite cartoon characters are Tom and Jerry. I love both of them. Tom is a domestic cat, and Jerry is a mouse who lives in the same house. They are both very funny and sweet. Tom is grey in colour and Jerry is brown. I watch the Tom and Jerry show on television and also have their CDs. I also have stuffed figures of Tom and Jerry.

Tom and Jerry are an absolute delight to watch. Their endless attempts to trouble each other are amazing. They are always upto some mischief or the other. Tom loves to set up traps to catch Jerry, and Jerry is always thinking of ways to steal goodies from Tom.

Although they keep fighting with each other, they are best of friends. They stand by each other whenever either of them needs help. They are a good example of friendship.

They are the most popular cartoon characters. They fight a lot but never harm anyone. I love watching their shows.

63 MY SUPER HERO

Spiderman is my super hero. He is very strong and powerful. He can climb up any wall like a spider. He can also swing from one place to the other with the help of webs. He wears a red and blue costume and keeps his face covered. He fights against bad men to protect the weak and innocent.

Spiderman's real name is Peter Parker. He lives with his Uncle Ben and his Aunt. He studies in a school like you and me. His biggest enemies are the Green Goblin and the Sand Man. I like him because he fights against evil to protect his loved ones.

I have collected many pictures of my super hero. I have put some of them on my

room walls and I have pasted some in my scrapbook. I never miss any of his shows on television. I wish I could be as strong as him and fight all the evil doers.

64 TRAFFIC RULES

Traffic rules are very important for our safety. In big cities and towns there are many vehicles and so it is important to follow the traffic rules. If we follow traffic rules, we will be able to travel safely and avoid road accidents.

Whenever we cross roads, we should use the zebra crossing. We should wait till the traffic light shows the green signal for us

to cross the road. We should always look first towards the left, then towards the right and then again towards the left before crossing the road. We should always hold our parents' or an elder person's hands while crossing a road. We should never run across a road or a street.

While travelling in a car, we should

always follow the traffic signals. We should never jump the traffic signal. We should only move when the traffic signal is green. We should not drive very fast. We should always be very careful while driving.

65 HOUSE ON THE FOURTEENTH FLOOR

My sister lives in Mumbai. Her house is on the fourteenth floor. She lives near the sea. I love to go to her house. The city looks very different from her flat. From the balcony, the sea looks like a big lake. When I look down, I can see nearly the whole city. Cars and people on the roads look like toys. The houses in the distance look like doll houses. It feels scary to stand in the balcony at times.

On the fourteenth floor, the wind blows very strongly. At night the city looks beautiful.

The whole place lights up like a Christmas tree. I can see lights as far as possible. Against the black background, I can see moving lights of cars and buses. I love to visit my sister's house.

66 A Visit to an Amusement Park

This summer vacation when my cousins came to visit me, my father took us to the

nearby amusement park. It is called the Adventure Island. We were all very excited to go there. We reached the park in the afternoon. My father bought the tickets, and we went inside. Inside the park, there were different rides. We sat in one of the rides called the Umbrella Merry-Go-Round. It made us go round and round like an umbrella. We were scared but also excited. We shouted with joy.

After the ride, we came to a small place where there were many cars. These were called the Bumping Cars. We all sat in different coloured cars. The cars kept

bumping into one another and we laughed with joy. We played till our time got over. From there we went to take a ride on a train that took us all around the park. We then enjoyed various other rides. The place was great fun.

It soon became dark and all rides were shut down. We were very hungry by then. We sat in a café for sandwiches and juice. We came back home before dinner time. It was a wonderful day.

67 MY FIRST DAY AT SCHOOL

I still remember my first day at school. I left a little early with my parents. Never having seen the inside of a school, I was very scared and nervous. I held my mother's hand very tightly. When we reached the school, my father filled all the forms. Then

we were asked to meet the principal. The principal was a very kind lady. She greeted us with a warm smile. I liked her from the very first moment. She asked me my name and also shook hands with me. She then called my class teacher. She too looked kind and friendly.

She took me to my class. The class was full of students like me. My teacher introduced me to the whole class. All the students greeted me and welcomed me to the new school. I sat in the front row, and soon made new friends. After the first day, I was never scared to go to school again. I love going to school now.

68 Cleanliness is Healthiness

Cleanliness is healthiness. We should always keep ourselves and our environment clean. We can keep many illnesses away by keeping our body and surroundings clean.

We should brush our teeth regularly in the morning and night. We should also have a bath every day. We must clean our body with soap. It helps us to keep the germs away. We must wear clean clothes. Our clothes must be washed regularly. We should always wash our hands before and after having our food. After playing we should always wash our hands and legs to get rid of the dirt.

We must always keep our rooms and our house clean. Our house should receive plenty of fresh air and sunlight. We should

also keep our neighbourhood and our city clean. We should never litter the roads or streets. If we keep ourselves and our surroundings clean, we can enjoy a healthy and happy life.

69 SAFETY AT HOME

Safety starts from home. We must always try and keep ourselves safe from accidents. By staying safe we can avoid getting hurt.

We should handle electrical appliances with care. We must never play with electrical appliances. We should not operate electrical items with wet hands. We should not play with washing machines and dish washer. In the kitchen we should keep ourselves away from the cooking range, gas cylinder and fire. We must not play with sharp things like knives, scissors and other tools.

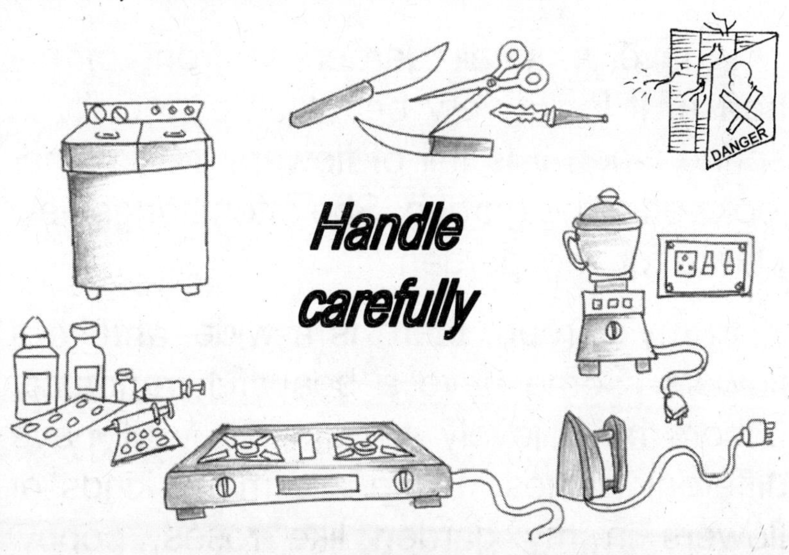

We should handle medicines carefully. We should not take any medicine without asking our parents. They can be very harmful and can make us ill. While staying alone at home, we should never open the door to strangers.

It is very important to follow all these safety measures at home.

70 FLOWERS IN MY GARDEN

I have a small garden in front of my house. It looks very beautiful, especially in spring when it is full of flowers. My mother looks after the garden. She often brings new plants for the garden.

In my garden, there is a wide variety of flowers. Some have a beautiful fragrance. Others have lovely colours. They all have different names. There are many kinds of flowers in my garden like roses, poppy, marigold, sunflower, gladioli, lily and many more. There is a small pond with a lovely fountain in the corner of my garden in which we have a few lotus flowers.

The flowers make my garden look very colourful and bright. Different types of birds and butterflies flutter around my garden. I love to play among the flowers. It makes me feel close to nature.

71 My School Bag

My school bag is blue in colour. My father bought me this bag on my last birthday. It has two loops on the back. My bag is quite spacious. It also has one flap in the front. I keep my notebooks in that flap. It has two side pockets where I keep my water bottle

and my lunch box. I can easily spot it among all other bags.

I carry my bag to school every day. My bag is very strong. I can say this because I carry loads of books in it every day. All my friends like my bag. But my bag has become old now. Some of its threads have come out. It has lost its shine. I still love my bag a lot. Even if my parents buy me a new bag, I will still keep the old bag with me.

72 LUNCH BREAK

In my school we have eight periods. After the first four periods, we have our lunch break. We all look forward to the break. As soon as the bell rings, we all rush out of our

classes. We carry our lunch boxes with us. After having our lunch, we rush to the school playground.

The school playground becomes very lively during the lunch break. All students play different games there. Some of my friends go to the school library during the lunch break. Some of them sit under the trees and chat. We play basketball and many other games like hide-and-seek and dumb-charades. We also meet our friends from other classes. During the lunch break we forget about our studies and just play. The lunch break gives us energy to get back to our studies again.

73 I AM A BLACKBOARD

I am a blackboard. I stay on the wall of a classroom. The name of the school is Mount Fort School. I am 50 inches in length and 30 inches in breadth. The classroom where I stay is beautiful and airy. Little children come to study in this classroom. I love to see them while they sit facing me for the whole day.

The classes start early in the morning. The teacher writes the date and day on the top left corner with the help of a chalk. She writes many things on me while teaching the children. I love to see the students attentively looking at the words written on me. When the teacher leaves the class, some of the children come and draw beautiful things on

me. They feel really happy to use me. Each year different children come to the class. I feel like their family member.

When the school gets over, I feel very lonely. The room becomes dark, and I hear no noise in the school. I eagerly wait for the next morning so that I can be with the children again.

74 HORSE RIDING

My uncle has a big stable on his countryside farmhouse. There are big horses in his stable. Last week I went to visit him. When I asked him to teach me how to ride a horse, he happily agreed. He took me to the stable the very next day. My uncle brought a small pony from the stable. He was light grey and white in colour. The pony was a little taller than me. I was afraid of the pony in the beginning.

My uncle helped me to ride the pony. He

told me how to hold the reins tightly. I felt very happy sitting on his back. After a few days, I could ride the pony all by myself. I named him Star. We soon became good friends. When it was time for me to go back home, I felt sad to leave Star behind. My uncle promised to take good care of Star till I visited the farmhouse again. This was my first horse riding experience.

75 MY COLOURING BOOK

I got a colouring book as a prize for winning a race in school. It is a big and thick book. It has nearly 200 pages. The name of my book is 'Colouring for Fun'. It is my favourite book. It has many pictures in it.

Some pictures are coloured and some are not. The book has different pictures. There are pictures of animals, birds, houses, trees and flowers. It also has pictures of my favourite cartoon characters.

I look into the coloured pictures and then colour the blank ones. Many a times I colour the pictures on my own but at times my mother helps me in colouring the pictures. I use my crayons to colour them. I carry my colouring book to school to show it to my teacher. She too helps me to colour the pictures in the book. I love this book a lot because colouring is an activity that I enjoy a lot.

76 My Uncle's Visit

Last week my uncle came to visit us after a long time. He is my father's distant cousin. He was to arrive in the evening. My father went to receive him at the airport. He was very tall and his suitcase was very big. He

had a big moustache. He had very little hair on his head and wore thick glasses.

In the beginning I felt shy talking to him. But slowly I realised that he was a very jovial person. I was very excited when he told me that he had travelled across the world. He told me stories of different places. I even asked my friends to come home to meet him. They were happy to hear his amazing stories. He stayed with us for three days, and those three days were full of excitement. I was sad on the day he left. Before leaving he promised to visit us again. He also gifted me a beautiful watch. He said that he was very happy to have a niece like me.

77 POLITENESS

To be polite means to show good manners and to respect others' feelings. Politeness is a great quality. It is very important to be polite with others. If we are polite, everyone will be friendly with us.

It is easier to make people understand if we talk to them politely. People will appreciate our point of view if we talk politely.

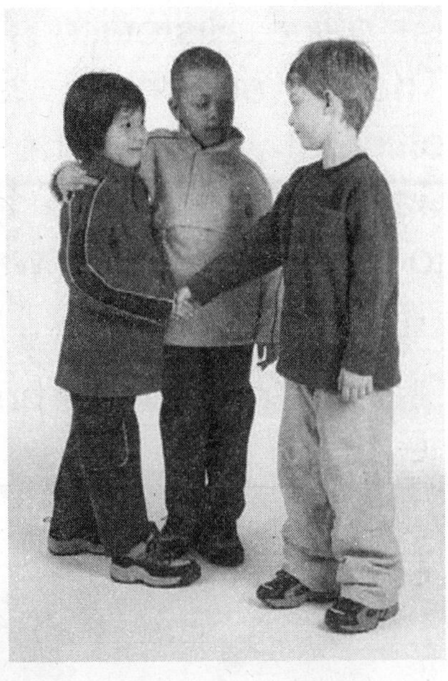

We should talk politely even to those whom we dislike. We should never use bad or harsh words for others. We should never get angry. We can calm down an angry person by talking to him or her politely. We should never be harsh even with animals. They too need love. We should be polite in handling them. Polite people are respected and loved everywhere and by everyone.

78

A Day in My Father's Office

Yesterday after school, I went to visit my father in his office. This was my first visit to his office. His office is in a very big building. There were many people working in the office. I went inside and saw my father waiting for me near the door. He took me to his cabin which was really big.

There were many people in the office. Staff members were hurriedly moving around

with files. Telephones were ringing. There were papers lying on every table. Some people were talking over on the phone, some were working on their computers and others were writing something in files. A huge pile of papers was kept on my father's desk. He had many books on his shelf. There was a fax machine, a telephone and a laptop on his desk. On the desk, there was a photo frame with a picture of me and my mother.

A few of his colleagues came to meet me. They were all very nice. One of them gave me some chocolates. I had lunch with my father, and then I went back home. I was very impressed with my father's office. I promised myself that I would grow up and work in an office like my father's.

79

My First Airplane Ride

During my last vacation, I went to visit one of my cousin brothers who is a pilot. I went to his training school to meet him. It was not very far from the hotel we were staying in. The training school was very big. It had three huge buildings and a big training ground. I was very excited to visit the place. My brother greeted me and took me to his room. There were pictures of different types of planes in his room.

When I asked my brother to give me a ride in a plane, he agreed. He took his chief trainer's permission and we went to the training ground. I was a little afraid at first, but when we started flying I was thrilled. We flew like the birds in the sky. I couldn't talk to my brother as he was wearing big headphones.

We flew over fields and houses. Everything looked so small from the plane! After some time I started feeling a little sick. So my brother landed the plane back to the ground. I was very proud of him. I loved my plane ride and now I too want to become a pilot like him.

80 Early to Bed and Early to Rise

Early to bed and early to rise makes a person healthy, wealthy and wise. We should follow proper discipline in our lives. This helps us to work hard by giving us energy. We should go to bed early at night, as this will help us to have proper sleep. Sleeping is very important to feel fresh in the morning.

We should also get up early in the morning. We will then have plenty of time to do all our morning exercises, to have our breakfast and get ready for school on time. If we sleep late at night, we cannot get up early in the morning. Proper sleep at proper time makes us active and energetic. We can then work hard and learn more. With good health and a sharp brain, we can always work hard to become successful.

81 MOHANDAS KARAMCHAND GANDHI

Mohandas Karamchand Gandhi was born on 2nd October, 1869 in Porbandar, a small town on the coast of Gujarat. He was a political and spiritual leader of India. He was a strict vegetarian and followed the path of non-violence. He always wore home-spun clothes and built a beautiful *ashram* on the banks of River Sabarmati in Gujarat.

The great poet Rabindranath gave him the title of 'Mahatma' or the *Great Soul*. After studying law in England, he returned to Mumbai and practised for a while. Then he went to South Africa where he was ill-treated for being a non-white. The hardships he faced there made him turn towards fighting injustice.

He returned to India and fought for the rights of the poor farmers. He also fought against untouchability and for the equality of women. He urged the people to lead a simple and disciplined life. He worked for the improvement of villagers. He encouraged the use of the goods made in the country instead of imported goods. The main weapons that he used to fight against the British were non-violence, non-cooperation and peaceful resistance. He protested against the rising prices of salt with Dandi march.

He was one of the greatest leaders of the Indian independence movement. He inspired people to follow the path of *ahimsa* or non-violence. He lead the civil disobedience movement against the British rulers. He wanted them to leave the country and give Indians complete freedom. He died on 30th January, 1948, having spent his entire life in service to the nation.

He will be remembered forever for his devotion and dedication to the cause of India's freedom struggle. The whole world still holds him in great respect. India has honoured him as the 'Father of the Nation' and many follow his teachings of *ahimsa*. His birthday, 2nd October, is celebrated as 'Gandhi Jayanti', a national holiday in India and as the 'International Day of Non-violence' worldover.

82 MOTHER TERESA

Mother Teresa was born on 26th August, 1910 in Albania. Though a Roman Catholic nun she took the Indian citizenship. She started the 'Missionaries of Charity' in Kolkata (Calcutta), and devoted her whole life to working for the 'poorest of the poor'. For over 45 years she served the poor, sick, orphaned and dying. At the age of 12, she felt that she was born to do God's work through helping the poor. She started to work

alone and without any funds. But soon people gathered around her as volunteers and many gave donations to support her good work. Today, her organisation, The Missionaries of Charity, provides help to the poor not only in India, but also in many parts of Asia, Africa and Latin America. They undertake relief work in the wake of natural catastrophes such as floods, epidemics and famines. In areas of war, her sisters have done a tremendous amount of work for the refugees.

Mother Teresa was honoured by both governments and civilian organisations. She was awarded the *Padma Sri* in 1962. She won the Nobel Peace Prize in 1979 for her humanitarian work. She was given the *Bharat Ratna* in 1980. When asked where she got the strength and perseverance to put her whole heart and soul into the service of others, Mother Teresa would simply answer—"In prayer."

Mother Teresa left this mortal world on 5th September, 1997, but her spirit lives on through the work she has done and the organisations that she began.

Eid

Eid is celebrated on a new moon night in April or May. It celebrates the breaking of the month-long fast, *Ramzan* and is celebrated by all Muslims with great enthusiasm and joy. *Ramzan* is the ninth month in the Muslim calendar and it is spent in fasting, feasting, worships and prayer. It is regarded as a highly auspicious month when Muslims unite for contemplation, spirituality and brotherhood. All Muslims fast each day of the month from dawn to dusk.

Those who are old or ill are exempt from observing a fast. Even children are exempt but many parents make the older children fast for a few hours.

On Eid, Muslims gather in large numbers to offer special prayers at mosques. People come out in new clothes and greet each other with “Id Mubarak.” They embrace each other and exchange sweets. Women of the house prepare a sweet dish from thickened milk and vermicelli, called *sevayian*.

Eid is the celebration of brotherhood and love among each other. It is also a festival that is meant to break the barriers between the rich and poor. Donating to the poor is also a part of the festival and Muslims do a lot of charity on this auspicious day. They give gifts in cash or kind to the poor and needy. Being a festival of joy and thanksgiving, people of other religions also join them. This is also a day to forget old ill-feelings towards fellow men and together celebrate the opportunities given by *Allah* (God).

84 DIWALI

Diwali is one of the major festivals of India. It is celebrated all over the country as Diwali, Kali Puja or Lakshmi Puja. It is also called the festival of lights and marks the victory of good over evil.

According to the *Ramayana*, when Lord Rama returned to Ayodhya after defeating Ravana, the people of Ayodhya welcomed him back by lighting their homes and streets with earthen oil lamps or *diyas*.

On this day people wear new clothes and decorate their houses with various types of earthen lamps and electric lights.

Many households pray to Goddess Lakshmi for the continued health, wealth and happiness of the family. Sweets are offered to God and then distributed amongst neighbours and friends. This day also has many people starting a new business or project.

The main entrance to the house is decorated with lights, *diyas* and *rangoli*. This is done not only to make the house beautiful but also give the visitors a warm welcome. It is customary for people to visit each others' house and exchange gifts.

The day before Diwali is celebrated as Dhanteras. It is considered auspicious to buy some metal as a symbol of wealth on this day. Some people buy gold and silver and some buy steel or copper utensils. The house is thoroughly cleaned, particularly the kitchen. All old and broken things are thrown away.

Diwali is celebrated as Kali Puja in West Bengal. This is the day when people pray to *Shakti* or the Mother Goddess. Early in the morning women decorate the floors with beautiful 'alpana'. The precious 14 earthen lamps are lit in memory of the ancestors.

No matter what form of prayers people follow, everyone awaits the fall of darkness. Suddenly the skyline lights up with the flare of crackers. They are in sharp contrast to the soft glow of the earthen lamps. Diwali is celebrated on a new moon day and the crackers are symbolically burst to dispel the darkness. But we should burst as less crackers as possible because crackers pollute the environment. We can also burst eco-friendly crackers. Diwali certainly does not mean creating pollution. Diwali is the time for old and young to come together and celebrate prosperity with food, clothes and lights.

STORIES

1

Slow and Steady Wins the Race

Once there lived a hare in a forest. The hare often laughed at the tortoise for his slow speed. The hare was very proud of his speed.

One day the tortoise challenged the hare for a race. The hare accepted the challenge, and the race started.

The fast hare soon went quite ahead of the tortoise. But when he was very near the finishing line, he thought, "Let me sit here under the tree and wait for the tortoise. When he comes, I shall run to the winning post before him. By this I will make him feel like a fool for having challenged me."

He sat under the tree and waited for the hare. But the tortoise was still far behind. After waiting for some time, the hare fell asleep. When he woke up, he saw the tortoise crossing the winning line.

The hare, because of his pride, lost the race. The tortoise won the race because he moved towards his goal 'slowly but steadily'.

2

United We Stand Divided We Fall

Once upon a time, four sheep lived together on a farm. They were very close friends. They stayed together and lived happily and peacefully. Whenever any wild animal attacked them, they all fought the enemy together and drove it away.

A wolf had an eye on these sheep. But he never dared to attack them as long as they were together.

One day the sheep fought and their friendship fell apart. Each one of them went in a separate direction. The wolf saw them and thought it to be a golden chance. He attacked the sheep one by one and ate them up.

As long as the sheep were united, they were happy and safe. But when they got divided, the wolf could easily kill them.

3 Where There is a Will There is a Way

It was a very hot day. A crow was feeling very thirsty. Its mouth was very dry, and its throat was burning. It flew from one place to another in search of water. But it could not find even a single drop of water anywhere.

At last the crow found a pot near a house. Peeping inside, he saw a little water at the bottom of the pot. The crow could see the water but could not reach it.

Suddenly an idea struck him. He started picking up stones from the ground and dropping them into the pot one by one. Slowly the water rose to the top and the crow could reach it easily. He happily drank the water and flew away.

4

IT'S GOOD TO BE KIND AND HUMBLE

One day a lion was sleeping outside his den. A little mouse who lived in a hole nearby came out to play. It played and ran all over the lion's body.

The lion woke up from his sleep and caught the mouse. The mouse begged the lion to let it go. It squeaked in a feeble voice, "Please let me go! Oh, kind King of the forest have mercy on me! I will repay your kindness one day."

The lion was very amused with what the mouse had said. He wondered how a little mouse could ever help the King of the forest. However, he took pity on the mouse and let it go.

After a few days, the mouse heard the lion roaring in pain. It ran to the lion and found him caught in a hunter's net. The lion was trying hard to free himself but to no avail. The mouse at once jumped to his help. It began to nibble the net with its sharp teeth. Soon the lion was free from the hunter's net. He thanked the little mouse for saving him.

5 TIT FOR TAT

Once upon a time, a fox invited a crane for dinner. He prepared a delicious soup for dinner. He served the soup to the crane in a plate. "Let us start our dinner," said the fox and started lapping up his soup.

The crane could smell the delicious soup, but he could not have even a drop of it. The crane's beak was too long while the plate

was very shallow. He knew that the cunning fox had played a trick on him. The crane just looked helplessly while the fox finished his soup.

A week later the crane invited the fox to dinner. He too prepared a delicious soup. Now the crane served the soup in a pot with a narrow neck.

"Please let us have the soup," said the crane and put his long neck into the pot.

He started sipping and praising the soup. "I have specially prepared the soup for you," said the crane to the fox. "Please have it, and don't feel shy."

But this time the fox could not have the soup. He was very hungry but the mouth of the pot was too narrow. He realised his mistake and promised never to play such a mean trick again.

6 Looks are Often Misleading

A stag was once very proud of his antlers. He used to look at his reflection in the river and think, "How beautiful are my antlers. No animal looks so beautiful."

Though he was proud of his antlers, he was always upset because of his legs. He thought of them as very thin and ugly.

One day a tiger chased the stag. The stag ran as fast as he could. Soon he entered a thick jungle. Now he had left the tiger far behind. He slowed down and started moving through the thick undergrowth very carefully. But his antlers soon got caught in the low hanging branches of a tree. He struggled very hard to free himself. But all his efforts went in vain.

The stag thought, "I always used to curse my ugly legs, but today they helped me to

run away from the tiger. I was so proud of my antlers, but now I am trapped because of them."

Soon the tiger caught up with the stag. He sprang on the stag and killed him.

7 THE DONKEY AND THE DOG

In a far away village, a donkey and a dog worked for a potter. The dog protected his master's pots and home. The donkey carried heavy pots to the market for his master.

The donkey was very jealous of the dog. He thought, "The dog lives such an easy life. He only has to stroll in the compound and bark at strangers. The master loves him more and gives him good food. As for me, I have to carry heavy loads to the market. The master beats me and gives me stale food."

So he thought of a plan to take over the dog's place.

The donkey noticed that the dog barked a little when the master returned home.

Then wagging his tail, he used to go to the master and put his front paws on his shoulders.

Next day when the master came back home, the donkey brayed a little, and then wagging his tail, he went to the master and put his front paws on his shoulders. Seeing the donkey's unusual behaviour, the potter got scared. Thinking that his donkey had gone mad, he rained heavy blows on him. The poor donkey got badly beaten that day.

8 Better be Hungry than in Chains

Once upon a time, a wolf came to a farm. There he met a farm dog. The dog was very healthy. The wolf, on the other hand, was thin and weak.

The wolf wondered how the dog was so

healthy. He asked the dog the secret of his health. The dog said that he looked after the farm and the master fed him well. He advised the wolf that if he works honestly, the master would feed him well too.

While talking to the dog, the wolf noticed a chain tied around the dog's neck. The other end of the chain was tied to a peg on the ground. He was curious to know about the chain, so he asked the dog about it. The dog replied that during the day his master kept him tied with the chain. The wolf got very scared. He said, "I would rather starve to death than be a slave to anybody."

Saying this, the wolf ran back into the forest.

9 THE HORSE AND THE DONKEY

One day, a man took a horse and a donkey to market. The donkey carried a heavy load on its back while the horse had nothing on his back.

On the way to the market, the donkey pleaded with the horse to share its burden. The horse replied, "It is your load. You should carry your own burden. I will not share it."

The donkey was sad and tired, but it said nothing to the horse. They both kept walking towards the market. After sometime the donkey could not carry the heavy load any more. It sank down on the road and its mouth started foaming.

Seeing the donkey's condition, the man removed the entire load from the donkey's back and placed it on the horse's back. Now the horse realised its mistake.

The horse thought, "I did not share the heavy burden with the donkey. Now I have to carry the entire burden all by myself. I shouldn't have been so selfish."

That day the horse learnt a lesson and since then he never refused to help others.

10 Jack of all Trades But Master of None

One day a fox and a cat were discussing wolves. They were both afraid of wolves. The fox said, "I know a lot of tricks to run away from the scary wolves. They are fast runners, but they cannot catch me."

The cat asked the fox about the tricks he knew. The fox replied, "I can run along the thorny hedge, hide in thick bushes, cover myself in burrows and there are many other tricks I know."

The cat in turn replied, "I only know one trick."

The fox was amazed to hear it and said, "It's sad that you know only one trick. But what is this one trick that you know?"

Before the cat could reply, a pack of wolves attacked both of them. The cat climbed up a nearby tree. There it was safe from the wolves. The fox tried one trick after the other but could not escape from the wolves.

The cat thought that its mastery over one trick was better than all the tricks of the fox. The fox was indeed a 'Jack of all trades but master of none'.

11 THE WIND AND THE SUN

One day the wind and the sun had a fight. The wind said that he was stronger than the sun. The sun said, "No, I am stronger than you."

A traveller was passing by at that moment. He had wrapped a shawl around him. The sun and the wind decided that whoever could make the traveller remove his shawl would be declared the strongest.

The wind took the first chance. He started blowing with all his might to remove the shawl from the traveller. But the harder he

blew, the tighter the traveller held his shawl around his body. The struggle went on till it was the sun's turn to try. The sun smiled warmly. The traveller felt the warmth of the sun and loosened his grip on the shawl. The sun smiled more warmly. Now the traveller started feeling hot. The sun's smile became warmer and warmer till the traveller could no longer keep his shawl around his shoulders. He took it off and put it in his bag.

Thus, the sun was declared stronger than the wind.

12 The Villager's Spectacles

Once there lived an illiterate villager. He did not know how to read or write. But he often saw his fellow villagers wearing spectacles and reading books. He thought that if he wore spectacles, he too would be able to read like his fellow villagers. So he decided to go to the town and buy spectacles.

He went to the town and entered an optical shop. He asked the shopkeeper to show him some reading glasses. The shopkeeper showed him various pairs of spectacles and also gave him a book to read. The villager tried all the spectacles one after the other but could not read the book. After trying on many spectacles, the villager told the shopkeeper that all the spectacles in his shop were useless. The shopkeeper gave him a doubtful look and asked him why he thought them all to be useless.

The villager said that even after wearing the spectacles, he could not read anything. The shopkeeper noticed that he was holding the book upside down. He asked the villager if he could read. The villager said he couldn't read. He wanted to buy the spectacles so that he could read. On hearing this, the shopkeeper laughed and said that spectacles will not help him to read. He must first learn how to read and write.

13 THE JOVIAL KNIGHT

Many years ago, there lived a knight. He was a very brave man. He had shown much

bravery in battles. He was a great horserider and a very good swordsman. He was a very kind man too. He helped the poor and the needy, and fought for the weak. He was loved and admired by all.

The knight had one secret that no one knew, not even his closest friends. He was bald! He wore a wig to cover his head. The wig was so perfect that no one knew about his baldness.

One day, the knight went hunting with his friends. Suddenly a gust of strong wind blew away his hat along with his wig. His friends were amused to find him bald and started laughing at him. They all asked him why he hid his baldness from them.

The knight jovially laughed along with them and said, "Yes, I did hide my baldness from all. But I was sure that one day everyone will know the truth. After all when my own hair did not stay with me, how can someone else's hair stay with me forever?"

On hearing this, all his friends felt ashamed at having laughed at him and said, "You are truly a great man."

14

Try! Try! Till You Succeed

Once upon a time there lived a king in Scotland. His name was Robert Bruce. He was a brave and kind-hearted king. He had been victorious in many battles, but once he got defeated in a battle and had to run away from the battlefield. He ran into a forest and found a cave where he took shelter.

Inside the cave, King Bruce saw a spider. It was trying to spin a web in the cave. But

each time it started to spin the web, the wind blew it off. After every failed attempt, the spider tried again. It did not lose hope. Finally the spider was able to spin its web.

This taught King Bruce a great lesson. He learnt that one should never lose hope and keep trying till one succeeds. The spider had given him new courage and hope. He came out of the forest and decided to fight his enemy. This time he fought very bravely and won his kingdom back.

15 The Grocer and The Fruit Seller

One day, a grocer went to borrow a weighing balance from the fruit seller. The fruit seller gave his balance to him. After a few days, the fruit seller went to the grocer to ask for his balance. But the grocer was a dishonest man. He said, "I am very sorry dear friend, but the mice ate up your balance. I cannot return it to you."

The fruit seller got very angry. But controlling his anger he said, "Never mind. I cannot blame you if the mice ate it." Saying this he left the grocer's shop.

One month later, the fruit seller came to the grocer. He asked him if he could take the grocer's son to the town to do some shopping. The grocer gave his consent. Next day, the fruit seller returned from the town all alone. The grocer got very worried and asked him about his son. The fruit seller said, "A crane took your son away."

The grocer got very angry and shouted,

"How can a crane carry away such a big boy!" The fruit seller very calmly replied, "Just the way mice ate away my balance."

The grocer realised his mistake. He returned the fruit seller's balance. The fruit seller then brought the grocer's son back. He had been staying at the fruit seller's house all this while.

16 The Boy Who Cried 'Wolf'

Once in a village there lived a shepherd boy. He used to take his flock of sheep for grazing to the nearby forest in the morning and bring them back in the evening. But soon he got very bored with this daily routine. One day, he decided to play some trick on the villagers.

All of a sudden he started shouting, "Help! Help! Wolf! Wolf!"

The villagers heard the boy's cries and rushed to help him. But when they saw the shepherd boy, they found him laughing out loudly for having fooled them. They got very angry at this. They told the boy that lying like this would get him into trouble some day.

A few days later the shepherd boy once again played the same trick and shouted, "Help! Help! Wolf! Wolf!"

The villagers once again rushed to help him. But when they found that the boy had tricked them again, they got very angry. They scolded the boy for being so naughty.

One day the wolf actually attacked the shepherd boy and his flock of sheep. This time when the boy cried for help, none of the villagers came to help him. After hearing the boy's cries for a long time, the villagers at last came to his help. But it was too late! When they reached the forest, they found the wolf had already killed a number of sheep and even wounded the shepherd boy.

17 Greed is a Curse

A poor farmer lived in a village. He lived his life with great difficulty. He earned very little and could hardly manage two meals a day.

One day, he came across a man who gave him a hen. The farmer was very puzzled, but he still took the hen.

Next morning, the farmer was very surprised to find that the hen had laid a golden egg. He sold the egg in the market and happily returned home. The hen laid a golden egg every day. Slowly the farmer became a rich man. But with time he grew greedier. He wanted to become the richest man in the village.

One day the farmer thought that there was a storehouse of gold eggs inside the hen. He wanted to get all the eggs at once. So he took a knife and cut open the hen's stomach. But to his surprise he could not find a single egg inside. Because of his greed, he had not only lost the golden eggs but also the hen forever.

18

Be Happy with What you are

Once upon a time there was a crooked tree in a forest. It used to feel very ugly because of its crooked trunk and branches. It used to envy all other fellow trees that were straight and fine looking.

One day a woodcutter came to the forest to cut some wood. When he came across the crooked tree, he thought, "This tree is useless for me, so I will not cut it."

He went to the other fine looking trees

and cut them all down. The crooked tree felt grateful to God for making it crooked. It never again felt ugly. It realised that because of its ugliness, it was saved from the axe of the woodcutter.

19 Cleverness Does Not Always Pay

Once upon a time, there lived a salt merchant in a village. He had a donkey on whom he would put heavy sacks of salt to

carry to the market. The salt sacks used to be very heavy for the donkey to carry.

One day while crossing the river, the donkey slipped into the water. When the donkey came out of the river, it realised that the load had become lighter. It felt very happy. Next day, the merchant again put heavy sacks of salt on the donkey's back. This time the donkey intentionally slipped into the river. The merchant understood its trick. He decided to teach the donkey a lesson.

Next day, he put a sack of cotton instead of salt on the donkey's back. The donkey did

not know about this, and it tried its old trick to make its load lighter. But this time the cotton became heavy after soaking in the water. The donkey could hardly come out of the river because of the heavy weight of the wet cotton. The donkey realised its mistake and learnt a good lesson. It never tried the trick again.

20 Riches do not Always Bring Happiness

Once there lived two mice. One lived in the countryside and the other lived in the town. Both of them were good friends. One day the country mouse invited the town mouse for dinner. He served the best berries, nuts and roots available in the countryside. But the town mouse on having the dinner said, "Your food is so tasteless and poor. You must come to the town to have good food with me."

On hearing this, the country mouse accepted his invitation.

Next week, the country mouse visited the town mouse. His friend served him figs,

honey, biscuits, bread and jam. The food was really good and tasty. But the two friends could not have their dinner in peace. Very often the cat would come and attack the two friends. The house of the town mouse was also very small and uncomfortable.

After dinner, the country mouse told his friend, "What a sad life you lead! In my house, I can at least eat and sleep in peace."

Saying this, the country mouse happily went back to his house in the countryside.